Visual Function

D0870869

For my father,
who prepared the content
but did not live
to see the form

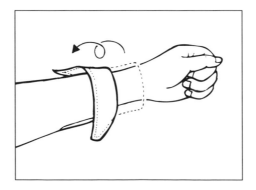

Visual Function

An Introduction to Information Design

Paul Mijksenaar

Princeton Architectural Press

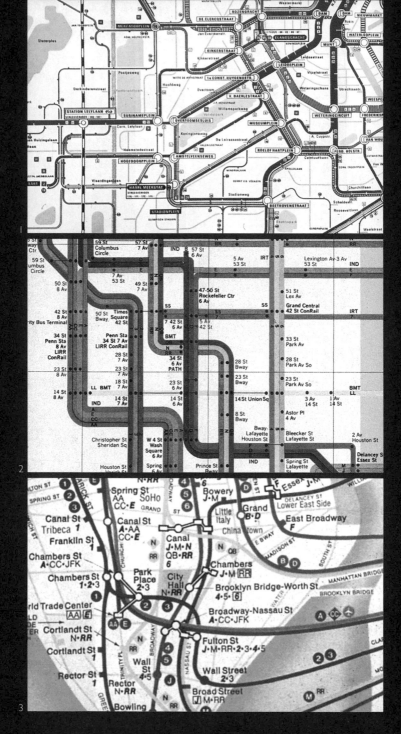

Example 1

Matches are tricky to use in a car and a pocket lighter dangerous. Car manufacturers have consequently come up with a special car lighter. But in the film 'Mon Oncle' the driver hands this gadget to his passenger (played by Jacques Tati as Monsieur Hulot) as if it were a match.
The designer had not foreseen that Monsieur Hulot would, in characteristic fashion, persist in throwing the thing out of the open car window.
The design should have offered more visual information – although in this particular instance a long chain attached to the lighter might have proved more effective.

1 Diagrammatic Amsterdam City Transport map, 1989–91.
2 Diagrammatic map of New York City Subway, 1977–78.
3 Diagrammatic map of New York City Subway, 1979 onwards.
4 Still from Jacques Tati's film *Mon Oncle*, 1958.

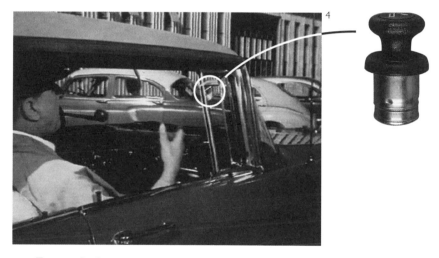

Example 2

In 1989 the graphic designer Hans van der Kooy devised a diagrammatic route map for the Amsterdam City Transport Authority. The design even received a national award for 'good industrial design'. Yet within two years management had withdrawn the map from circulation because neither passengers nor personnel could make head or tail of it. Both designer and management should have known better. After all, a similar problem had already arisen in 1977 with Massimo Vignelli's map of the New York subway: it was replaced in 1979 by a topographic map designed by John Taurenac. During the same period a research group at Delft University of Technology engaged in studying the effectiveness of the famous diagrammatic map of the London Underground (designed in 1933 by the technical draughtsman Henry Beck) had offered possible reasons for the success of the topographic approach in its final report.[17] When reality is radically schematized, the link with that same reality is quickly lost. For metro-type systems with few stops and long distances in-between, this is not so much of a problem. But in the case of fine-meshed transport systems like tram and bus networks, it is vitally important to retain a recognizable reality – which is why London Transport uses a different kind of map for its bus network, one that looks much more like an ordinary street plan. The numerous route numbers are shown in large circles at all major intersections, thereby making it possible to follow the complicated bus routes quickly and easily. This idea, incidentally, came from a British architect – Andrew Holmes – rather than a graphic designer.[14] Although the merits of the London Underground Map are beyond question, the Delft study group demonstrated, with the aid of its

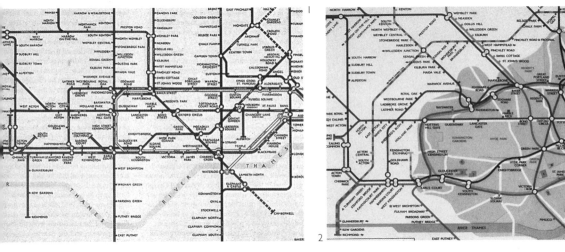

1 One of the many variations of Henry Beck's *diagram* of the London *Underground*, said to be Beck's own favorite[6] (poster format), 1949.
2 The Delft design.

own design, that the best solution is sometimes a compromise that involves combining the strong points of different concepts. In the Delft version, underground routes in the center of London are rendered topographically, those outside diagrammatically. In the city center the map is augmented with references to major landmarks like parks, places of interest, and museums. This enables tourists, for example, to plan their visit better and avoid bizarre detours.

Example 3
In 1986 the space shuttle Challenger exploded shortly after lift-off at Cape Canaveral, killing all seven astronauts on board – a dramatic event that dealt a severe blow to the American space program. The probable cause was a defect in a sealing ring, to be precise, a rubber O-ring. In its

17 Source reference, see page 54

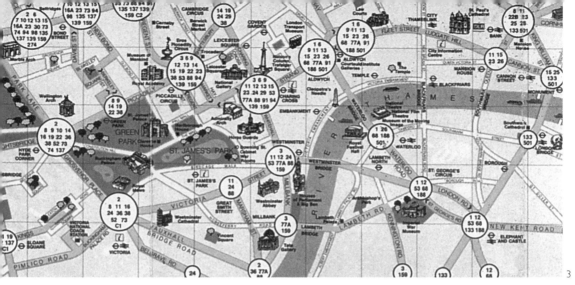

3

report on the disaster, the investigative committee included a graph tracing defects in these rings during earlier launchings. On those occasions, fortunately, they had been discovered in time. The graph notes the prevailing atmospheric temperature for each launching. Edward Tufte, professor of statistics, graphic design, and political economy – all three at Yale University, no less – contends that a clearer presentation of these same facts would have revealed a link between defective O-rings and low temperatures. Since the forecast temperature on that disastrous January day was lower than for any previous flight, namely 31 degrees Fahrenheit (half-a-degree Celsius below freezing), extrapolation of the graph might well have averted the disaster. [23]

3 Recent London Transport bus map for the center of London.
4 Graph produced by the committee investigating the space shuttle *Challenger* disaster.
5 Improved version proposed by Edward Tufte.

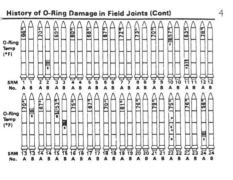

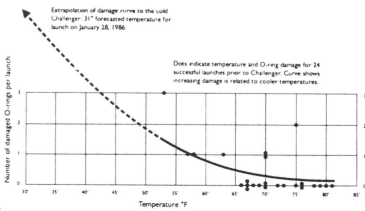

5

Example 4

The entrances to the former Maliebaan railway station in Utrecht, now the Railway Museum, and to the former 'Gemeentetram' administration offices in Amsterdam, date from an age when architecture provided clearly identifiable entries to buildings, often giving them fine and appropriate lettering as well – as above the Bungehuis entrance in Amsterdam. Our own age has produced the entrance to a student residence in Amstelveen. The only clue to its function is the large number of bicycles nearby. As for the inscrutable entrance to the Rotterdam Kunsthal, designed by Rem Koolhaas, it is soon to be moved...

1 'Gemeentetram' entrance
  in Amsterdam designed
  by City architect Marnette
  in 1922.
2 Entrance to *Uilenstede*
  student residence in
  Amstelveen, built in the
  1950s.
3 *Bungehuis* entrance in
  Amsterdam, designed by
  W.J. Klok in 1934.
4 The *Railway Museum* in
  Utrecht, formerly a railway
  station, dates from 1874.

2

3

4

1

2

3

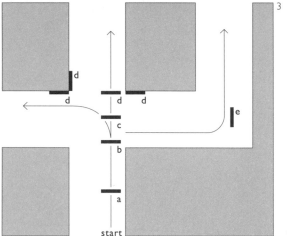

4

1 Striking entrance to the
  Opéra de Paris Bastille.
2 Façade lettering above the
  entrance to the hospital.
3 Diagram showing various
  options for the placement
  of directional signs within
  a building.
4 The goods entrance of an
  industrial building. The
  main entrance is around
  the corner!

Although a change is discernible among the new generation of architects, they still seem to have trouble making functions recognizable on the outside of buildings and making the spaces inside easy to find.
This despite the fact that it is already possible to pinpoint the places where visitors are going to need information (diagram) during the design phase of a building. More importantly, an efficient structure can do away with the need for information about routes and destinations altogether.

The previous examples concerned designers with an inaccurate or inadequate insight into usefulness, whose conceptual model was faulty if you like.[20] A second series of examples shows how designers sometimes wittingly diminish the practical value of their product by putting aesthetic criteria ahead of usefulness.

In the diagram:
start
a
b
c
d
d
d
d
e

Example 5
The Swatch wristwatch helped revitalize the Swiss watch industry, but it is so difficult to read that we need to allow extra time if we want to be sure that we'll catch our train or be on time for a lecture.

Example 6
For those who need to be able to read the time, there are readily available alternatives to the Swatch watch, but sometimes the consumer has no choice. The designer often seems only too happy to sacrifice the text to his artistic aspirations. Contemporary graphic design is rife with examples of design overkill.

5

SCHONE SCHIJN

Naar buiten toe wordt (en werd) een wereldtentoonstelling gepresenteerd als een uiting van verbroedering der volkeren. De thema's van recente expo's zijn daarin duidelijk. Het gaat om vooruitgang, perspectieven voor de mensheid, ontdekkingen.
Bij nadere beschouwing blijkt ook sprake te zijn van strijd tussen de landen binnen het tentoonstellingsterrein als daarbuiten. Binnen de tentoonstelling betwisten deelnemers elkaar medailles, getuigschriften en oorkonden die worden toegekend aan goede en betere produkten. De landen zich individueel gaan presenteren concentreert zich (onder meer) op de paviljoenen. Welk land heeft het grootste, hoogste, indrukwekkendste gebouw? Elk land zichzelf respecteert doet een goed naar de ereplaatsen. Tot aan de Tweede Wereldoorlog werben koloniale mogendheden (waaronder Nederland) binnen de stand. Hele kampongs en kralen worden gebouwd, vergaapt zich aan koloniale onderdrukkers maken indruk met aankleiding toe de discussie over het fenomeen wereldmisdaad. Tot en met de grootste internationale des Expositions BIE p goedgekeurd ten toen is de strijd voor tussen plekken en een woordtentoonstelling te mogen organiseren ook de Publiciteit geroemd de expo zo'n geweldig evenement dat ten ervan gebruik maken hun ongenoegen te uiten over de maatschappij.
Verbroedering: schone schijn.

6

5 Three models from a range of hundreds of different *Swatch* wristwatches.
6 Page from Grafisch Nederland, an annual PR publication put out by the Royal Association of Dutch Graphic Companies.
7 'Semi Sans' typeface designed by Anne Bastien.

abcdefghijklm
nopqrstuvwxyz
ABCDEFGHIJKLM
NOPQRSTUVWXYZ
0987654321
(#@$?&)+ìàéïòï

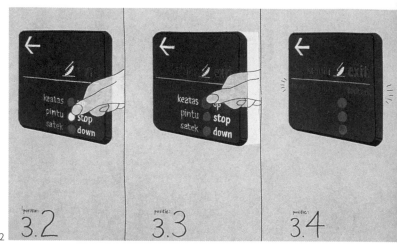

1

2

Example 7

1-4
Design studies for improving the locking procedure for the door of the *Fokker 50*. Original situation (1) and various studies for an electrical control panel (2), door handle (3), and operating instructions in the event that the existing door mechanism remained unchanged (4).

Around 1980 the aircraft manufacturer Fokker was having difficulties with its doors. Research showed that cabin staff unfamiliar with Fokker planes were baffled by the complicated locking procedure. The Delft University of Technology was asked to take a look at the operating instructions. Although the investigators demonstrated that these could indeed be improved, they also concluded that the real problem lay in the over-complicated locking mechanism; in other words, new visual instructions would be no more than a half-measure. Their advice, therefore, was to redesign the door. Their suggested solution focused on spatial design, moving part of the operating mechanism to an electrical control panel next to the door. Here, too, the university was able to suggest improvements based on a functional analysis.

3

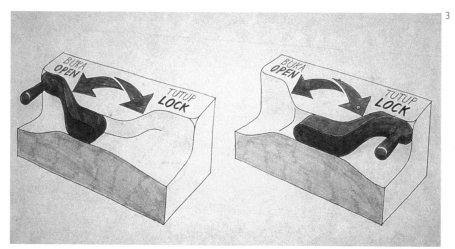

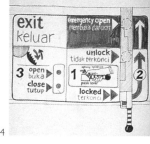

4

I shall close this introduction with a quotation from Donald Norman's 13 instructive and entertaining book *The Psychology of Everyday Things*:
'Many of the modern telephone systems have a new feature that automatically keeps trying to dial a number for you. This feature resides under names such as automatic redialing or automatic callback. I am supposed to use this feature whenever I call someone who doesn't answer or whose line is busy. When the person next hangs up the phone, my phone will dial it again. Several automatic callbacks can be active at a time. Here's how it works. I place a phone call. There's no answer, so I activate the automatic callback feature. Several hours later my telephone rings. I pick it up and say "Hello," only to hear a ringing sound and then someone else saying "Hello." "Hello," I answer. "Who is this?" I hear in reply, "you called me". "No," I say, "you called me, my phone just rang". Slowly I realize that perhaps this is my delayed call. Now, let me see, who was I trying to call several hours ago? Did I have several callbacks in place? Why was I making the call?'

Norman claims that the design of this telephone flouts an important design principle – visibility. The controls, as in so much modern equipment, perform multiple functions and there is a lack of 'feedback', meaning that users have no way of knowing whether their actions are producing the desired result. The multiple options are hidden from view, and there are a great many more of them than there are control buttons. This is in contrast to an automobile, for example, where most of the controls are visible and correspond fairly well to what they do. The advantage of this, according to Norman, is that the user has less to memorize.[20]

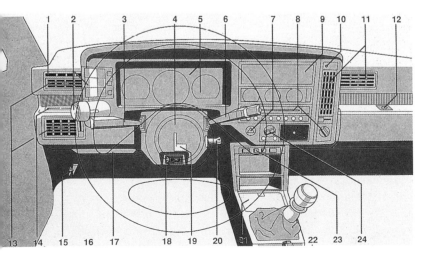

Dashboard controls in an automobile, from the owner's manual of a *Volvo 480*.

Form or Function?

So far we have been dealing with the design of visual information. Some of the aspects involved clearly belong to the neighboring worlds of industrial design, graphic design, morphology, and experimental psychology, with here and there a dash of business studies and construction. Nevertheless, for the sake of clarity when discussing education and research, it is advisable to define the territory of visual information as precisely as possible. Such a definition facilitates interdisciplinary collaboration. Designers have a tendency to combine values and principles discovered by other disciplines into a workable whole that adds up to more than the sum of its parts, or, as Josef Albers put it: in design 1 + 1 sometimes equals 3.[1] In view of countless earlier failures,

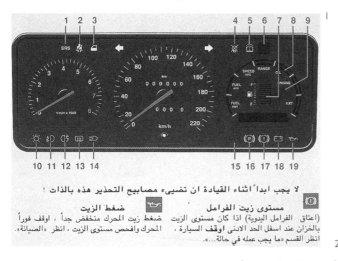

1 Analogue dashboard gauges in an automobile. Page from the Arabic version of the operating instructions for a *Volvo 480*.
2 Dynamic route map on the display of a *Bosch Travelpilot*, which can be mounted in any automobile. Other versions include spoken directions.

an attempt to determine just what constitutes design would seem to be a precarious and impractical undertaking, and likely to throw up more questions than answers. Perhaps this is also because – as Robin Kinross asserts in his excellent essay *Modern Typography* – abstract debate has its limits, and theories about design depend in part on their translation into real products.[13]

Designing what?

This question implies that designers 'do' what they do with something that already exists: just as a cook cooks with food and a gas stove, they work with information. This notion, however, is fast losing its meaning. Since all interpersonal communication involves information of one kind or another, it would be better to talk about designing instructions for using a product. This could be an appliance or a tool or, equally, a service or a facility. A product may itself provide visual information, such as a clock, a calendar, a street map, a graph, a route indicator, a computer. But over and above this, the actual use of a product may entail additional visual information, such as can be found on a keyboard, a control panel, or in operating instructions.

Which form?

Today's motto is very much: 'function can take any form'. The phrase is an adaptation of the famous, sometimes disputed credo, 'form follows function'. It crops up in every publication on this subject and the present one is no exception! It is usually attributed to the American architect Louis Sullivan, who introduced the proposition in a lecture

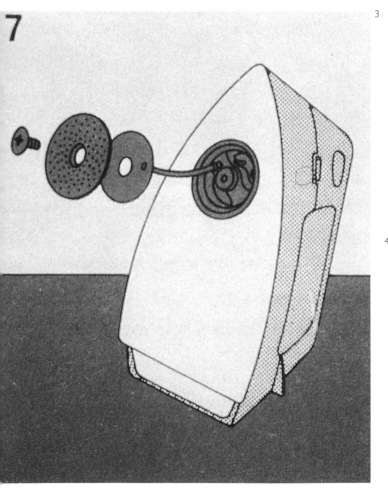

3

4

3 Detail from the operating instructions for a *Philips* steam iron.
4 Parking ticket dispenser in Paris.

given in 1896. In fact, historians trace it to Sullivan's fellow-American, the sculptor Horatio Greenough, who had used it in *Form and Function*, written in 1851.[2] Writing about the beauty of ships (he was thinking specifically of those superb, early-nineteenth-century motorized sailing ships the clippers), Greenough stated that it 'has been effected, first, by strict adaptation of forms to functions, second, by the gradual elimination of all that is irrelevant and impertinent'. Beauty was thus equated with functionalism.[10] Commenting on this, the author of the book *Industrial Design*, John Heskett, remarked that 'Clipper ships were certainly among the most beautiful creations of their age, but Greenough tended to ignore the degree of scientific calculation that went to determining their form, and the particular functional objectives for which they were designed. They were built for the opium trade with

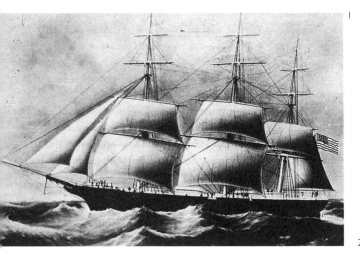

1 American clipper ship *Cowper*, 1854.
2 Passenger's cabin on the liner *Imperator*, 1913.
3 The *Titanic*. The huge, slanted funnels were dictated largely by aesthetic considerations.

China, in which speed was necessary to evade government patrols and pirates alike; . . . Calculations concerned with speed thus dictated the form of the hull, overriding optimum requirements for the inner working-structure and the organization of the ship, and in this secondary area, function had to be adapted to form.'

Later on, Henry van de Velde and Le Corbusier praised these North Atlantic liners as examples of functionalism and of 'pure, neat, clear, clean and healthy architecture'. Nonetheless, such ships contained plenty of features that had nothing to do with utility. The size and number of funnels were deliberately chosen to create a powerful impression of grandeur. The interior was designed to please and above all reassure the passengers, and to divert their attention from less agreeable aspects like seasickness and the dangers inherent in any sea voyage. These, too, were important functions.[10]

Thus, confusion about the notions of functionalism and beauty is nothing new, for emotion and social and cultural needs also play a role in determining function. Many felt that a scrupulously honest approach to construction and materials would automatically take care of these needs. Frank Lloyd Wright was not alone in stating that 'the machine, with its tendency towards simplification, is capable of revealing the true nature and beauty of materials'. In 1992 Edward Tufte concluded anew that aesthetics are a happy by-product of the visual presentation of information.[23] 'Form', in other words, meant above all 'beauty', a notion that later appeared to fall into discredit, with beauty often being regarded as a bonus.

3

Design became first and foremost a tool for welding together construction and function. If the result was pleasing and showed good taste, the aesthetic dividend followed automatically. Walter Gropius, director of the Bauhaus, a school that cannot be omitted from this account, remarked in 1926 that designing houses and their interiors for the mass market was 'more a matter of ingenuity than of passion'. And in his conviction that the artistic designer should attend the same school as the technical designer and design engineer, he was forty years ahead of Delft University's Faculty of Industrial Design Engineering.'[9]

To the relief of many, it seems that 'beauty' can be successfully excluded from industrial design on the grounds of its alleged elusiveness. Yet designers know from experience that many rational issues play a role in the perception of beauty. One example noted by A. M. Bevers, professor

1

2

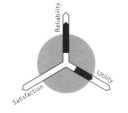

Falk map

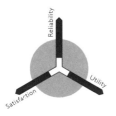

Michelin map

of Arts and Humanities at Erasmus University, Rotterdam, is the human preference for (or aversion to) symmetrical and geometrical forms: 'In the last instance, geometrical forms owe their aesthetic value to their useful, that is to say, structuring function. Perhaps we find something beautiful because it reminds us of the pleasure of an earlier experience, when something useful was experienced as pleasing. The experience of beauty has remained while the awareness of usefulness has disappeared.[3] 'This accords with the verdict of the Belgian architect, furniture designer, and graphic designer, Henry van de Velde (1863–1957) who said: 'Beauty is the result of clarity and system', adding, 'and not of optical illusion'.[27] The only conclusion possible is that design always involves three inextricably related elements, however much their relative proportions may differ from one application to the next, namely: durability, usefulness, and beauty. In this respect, design is an activity that unites the elements of durability and usefulness and intensifies the perception of beauty. Without noticing it, we have gone back almost two thousand years to the Roman architect Vitruvius. In his ten-volume treatise on architecture[12] he stipulated that it should satisfy the following criteria:

Firmitas *durability, firmness*
Utilitas *usefulness, commodity*
Venustas *beauty, delight*

I have attempted to turn these qualities into a practical three-point formula: Reliability, Utility, Satisfaction. What sort of combination of these qualities produces a good product? To measure this I have devised a simple, star-shaped diagram consisting of three thermometer-like axes that can be used to register the relative strength of the three criteria in any given product. The length of these thermometers is theoretically unlimited. Since none of these qualities should ever register zero in my opinion, this value has been excluded from consideration. A circle indicates an average level below which no good product should fall, although it may, of course, always do better. This diagram makes it possible not only to indicate in advance the precise mix of qualities required in a given product, but also to analyse existing products. Here, for example, are three comparisons I have worked out using the diagram:

- Dutch Falk street plans **versus** Michelin maps.
- Dutch road signs **versus** English road signs.

1 Wool mark, designed by
  Francesco Saroglia in 1964.
2 Version of the David star
  designed by Otto
  Treumann.
3 Dutch roadside route sign
  for local roads.
4 Roadside route sign in
  London giving through
  destinations. A little
  further on is a signboard
  of the same size giving
  local destinations.

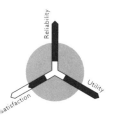

Dutch route signposting

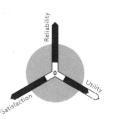

English route signposting

3

4

Swatch wristwatches

Extending coffee measuring spoon

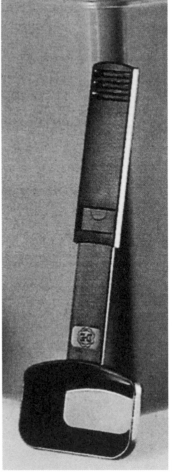

1

2

• An extending measuring spoon for coffee from the largest Dutch coffee concern, Douwe Egberts (Sara Lee), **versus** a Swatch watch

The advantage of this graphic form, apart from the fact that it allows priorities to be established for individual products, is that it is not susceptible to the kind of dogmas that may arise from too narrow an interpretation of functionality on the one hand, and of design on the other hand. What do I mean by dogmas in this context? Two examples will suffice: in 1920 Walter Portsmann, a German engineer, published a dissertation entitled *Sprache und Schrift* (Speech and Writing) in which he pointed out the advantages – chiefly greater efficiency – of using only *Kleinschreibung*, or lower-case, letters. The rationality of this work appealed to the imagination of the graphic designers of his day. They

10. 25. 500
din a 4
bauhaus
bayer

wir schreiben alles klein, denn wir sparen damit zeit
außerdem: warum 2 alfabete, wenn eins dasselbe erreicht?
warum groß schreiben, wenn man nicht groß sprechen kann?

3

adopted his ideas but in the process they added their own ideological gloss: in abolishing capital letters they were also abolishing one of many superfluous hierarchies. In 1925, the Bauhaus officially abolished the use of capitals. [13] The measure was explained in the lower-left-hand corner of the writing paper designed for the school by Herbert Bayer: 'we write everything in lower case because it saves time; besides, why have 2 alphabets if one achieves the same purpose? why write in capitals when we cannot speak in capitals?' At the same time the Bauhaus introduced the DIN A4 paper size and applied the 1924 DIN standard (no. 676) for the layout of writing paper. This dogma was later adopted by many Dutch designers including Piet Zwart, Willem Sandberg and the designers of the Amsterdam consultancy Total Design, who were still sticking resolutely to small letters when they designed the signage system for Amsterdam's

1 Flamboyant Swatch watch from the studio of the architect *Allessandro Mendini.*
2 Douwe Egberts extending measuring spoon.
3 The lower section of the writing paper designed by Bauhaus teacher Herbert Bayer.
4 Two pages from *Experimenta typographica 2* by Willem Sandberg, 1969.

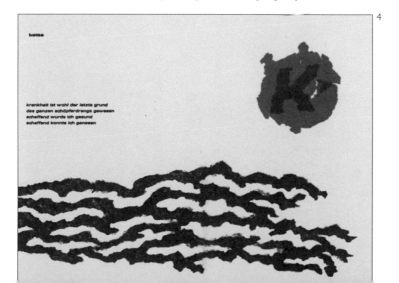

4

krankheit ist wohl der letzte grund
des ganzen schöpferdrangs gewesen
schaffend wurde ich gesund
schaffend konnte ich genesen

1 Signage at Schiphol airport designed by Total Design's Benno Wissing in 1967.
2 1963 test models from the Road Research Laboratory in England. Researchers found that place names in small letters with initial capitals (right) were easier to recognize.
3 Cartoon used by Ernst Gombrich in his article 'The Visual Image' showing the ambiguity of symbols. Charles E. Martin, drawing, © 1961, The New Yorker Magazine, Inc.
4 Enlarged detail of a reprint of the first red Michelin hotel guide from 1900, which already made use of symbols, mainly in order to save space.

new Schiphol Airport in 1967 – despite the fact that legibility research conducted in 1960 had shown what every typographer had long known, that the recognizability of names, especially in the kind of search operations involved in reading signposts and forms, increases significantly when each name or sentence begins with a capital letter. [16]
Another dogma of the period that saw the completion of Amsterdam's Schiphol Airport was that pictograms served only to produce communicative 'noise' and as such were inferior to what was, after all, perfectly unambiguous text. Yet the first red Michelin guide (hotels and restaurants) published in 1900 had already demonstrated the advantage of pictograms, namely their compactness. (Connoisseurs' attention is directed to the first line from the top, where a stylized symbol of the telegraph machine, designed by the Frenchman Claude Chappe, indicates

2

EXETER
KEIGHLEY
BRISTOL

Exeter
Keighley
Bristol

Morlaix (Finistère), ⬦SP⬦, 13,114 h., 🚂 ✉ ⌇.
Paris, 522 kil. — Plougonven, 10 kil. — Roscoff, 25 kil.
— Lannion, 36 kil. — Landerneau, 40 kil. — Châteaulin, 63 kil.
🏨 *** de l'Europe, rue d'Aiguillon. ACF
— * de Provence, place de Dossen. TC.F ◆
🔫 Huitric, rue Carnot, 11. Ⓐ Ⓜ
Ess.OL Berthou, rue Carnot, 10. Ⓥ Ⓦ Ⓢ
— Tanguy, Cycles, rue de Brest, 16. Ⓐ Ⓢ

Mormant (Seine-et-Marne), Ⓒ, 1,100 h., 🚂 ✉ ⌇.
TELEPH. 0 fr. 40 📧 ⚖
Paris, 53 et 58 kil. — Guignes-Rabutin ⚙, 9 kil. — Nan-

1 Toyota advertisement.
2-4
Use of pictograms on the remote control of a Philips television (2), Siemens appliances (3), and on a Dutch Rail sign board (4).
5-6
An example of their application (5) and a random selection of the pictograms introduced at Schiphol airport in 1993 (6). They are intended to reinforce the bilingual (Dutch and English) text.

the presence of a telex, and to the black diamond-shaped sign a few lines below this, indicating that the hotel has a darkroom.) Nevertheless, it was not until 1970 that Dutch Rail decided to introduce pictograms on a large scale in their station signage. They opted for a revised version of the standardized pictograms already adopted by the combined European railway companies and commissioned the Hague-based consultancy Tel Design (Gert Dumbar and Gert-Jan Leuvelink, among others) to design them.

Pictograms were also starting to appear in connection with various industrial products at this time. Among the pacesetters were Siemens (household appliances), Philips (audiovisual equipment) and Toyota (automobiles). Manufacturers had woken up to the distinct economic advantage of using pictograms in their instruction manuals: only one version for each product was needed. Henceforth consumers the world over received a multilingual booklet and the task of memorizing what all the little symbols meant. In the design of visual information in particular there is little room for eternal values, and the criteria change as easily as does consumer behavior. In May 1993 initial capitals were reinstated at Schiphol Airport and a large number of pictograms made their appearance. We return to the revised version of Vitruvius's three design virtues, combining design, reliability, and utility for the pleasure

2

3

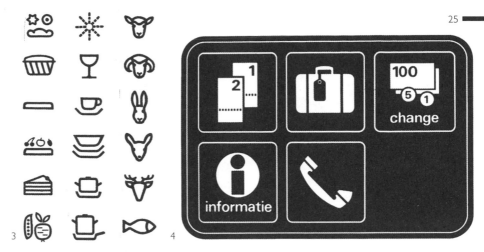

4

and satisfaction of users. Design after all has the unique capacity to shape information by

- emphasizing or understating
- comparing or ordering
- grouping or sorting
- selecting or omitting
- opting for immediate or delayed recognition
- presenting it in an entertaining fashion [22]

In general one can state that in the conceptual model, information should be as simple, clear, and unambiguous as possible. But when it comes to presentation, it can be enriched with a wealth of details, preferably applied at different levels. This way there is sure to be 'something for everyone'. [20]

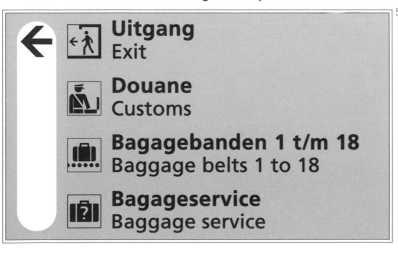

Uitgang
Exit

Douane
Customs

Bagagebanden 1 t/m 18
Baggage belts 1 to 18

Bagageservice
Baggage service

5

6

Een overheerlijke bramenmousse

1 Suiker toevoegen. Passeer verse, rijpe bramen door een zeef in een kom. Strooi er naar smaak fijne tafelsuiker op (boven) en roer grondig tot de twee ingrediënten goed zijn vermengd.

2 De room erdoor mengen. Sla slagroom met een garde stijf tot hij zachte pieken vormt. Schep de bramenpuree beetje bij beetje voorzichtig door de room (boven) Roer het mengsel tot het glad en gelijkmatig van dikte en kleur is.

3 De vla serveren. Schep hele bramen om met een weinig suiker, zodat ze zoet worden en het sap eruitloopt. Leg ze op bordjes, af, zoals hier, in hoge glazen. Vul de glazen met de vla (boven); werk ze af met een decoratieve krul (rechts). Koel de vla 2 uur en dien hem op. □

1 Illustration for a National Geographic magazine article about tropical rainforests.
2 Detail from the Time-Life cookbook series.
3 Two pages from the Mitchell Beazley book Man & Machines.

A few 'modern classic' examples of this approach are the Time-Life cookbook series, the Mitchell Beazley reference books, the Readers Digest handbooks, and the National Geographic Magazine. The challenge for researchers and designers is to continue to reveal the basic principles of design and to investigate whether it is possible to devise a common grammar for the transmission of information by means of picture and text.[29]

3

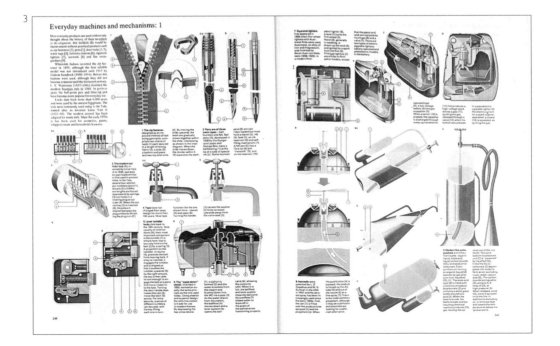

Visual Information

The first known graphical representation of change dates from the fourteenth century and is attributed to the bishop of Lisieux (c. 1320–1382), Nicholas Oresme, who is also reported to have suggested, long before Galileo, that the heavens move around a stationary earth. Oresme depicted data as vertical columns along a horizontal axis from left to right. The height of the vertical columns expresses intensity. The geometrical figure through the tops of the vertical columns indicates the change occurring in the chosen subject, for example over a certain period of time.[7] (The scientific definition of this system of horizontal and vertical axes had to wait until the seventeenth century when it was described by René Descartes. It subsequently became known as the

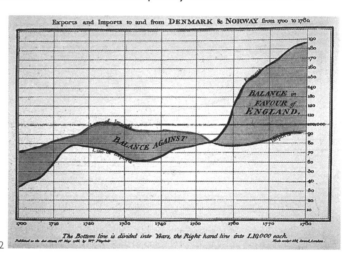

1 The very first graph depicting change, dating from the 14th century.
2 Graph depicting imports and exports between England and Denmark, drawn by William Playfair in 1780.

Cartesian coordinate system.) It was left to the English political economist William Playfair, who had started out as a draughtsman with James Watt, the inventor of the steam engineer, to realize that such graphical representations could be used to present not only empirical data but statistics of all kinds.[4] In the space of about a century, Playfair and others developed almost all the graphical forms we know and use today. During the Crimean War (1854–1855), the English nurse Florence Nightingale (1820–1910) devised a 'polar' graph with which she succeeded in convincing the Ministry of War that more soldiers were dying as a result of poor nursing than of injuries sustained during the fighting.[26]

One important historical example, produced by the French engineer Charles Joseph Minard (1781–1870), cannot go unmentioned here.

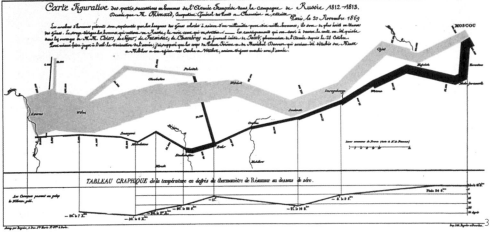

Edward Tufte, author of the impressive *The Visual Display of Quantitative Information*[24] and its sequel, *Envisioning Information*,[25] calls it possibly the best statistical graphic ever drawn. At the left of the graph Napoleon begins his march on Moscow (far right) with an army of 422,000 men. This is shown in beige. By the time he reaches his goal he has only 100,000 men left. During the return journey, represented by a black line from right to left, he sustains further substantial losses as a result of the intense cold (sometimes as low as thirty degrees [Celsius] below zero) and the arduous crossing of icy rivers. The temperature is depicted at the bottom in a separate, synchronous graph. The graph shows, for example, that during the crossing of the Berezina River with a temperature of minus twenty, Napoleon loses 22,000 soldiers! In the end only 10,000 men make it back to base. Minard's graph is a brilliant combi-

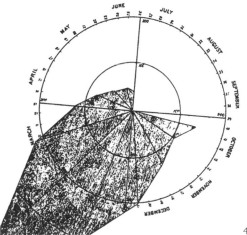

3 Minard's double graphic depicting Napoleon's disastrous Russian campaign (1812–1813).
4 Florence Nightingale's 'polar' graph. Within a circle representing a single year, she plotted the daily loss of life among the wounded during the winter of the Crimean War.

nation of statistical information (troop numbers and temperature variations) and topographical data (direction, distance, and location). Yet despite what many people think, graphical representations are less suitable for inexperienced readers. The fact is that they require a degree of intellectual training. Pictorial representations are not necessarily 'easier'; rather, they are more concise, more compact, clearer and, when well-done, more compelling.[25] These qualities were recognized by the Austrian economist Otto Neurath who, as director of the Vienna Gesellschafts und Wirtschaftsmuseum (Social and Economic Museum), introduced his Isotype method in about 1936. At the heart of his method was a 'visual dictionary' containing some two thousand symbols and a companion 'visual grammar', which made it possible 'to relay information in such a way that it can be grasped pretty well immediat-

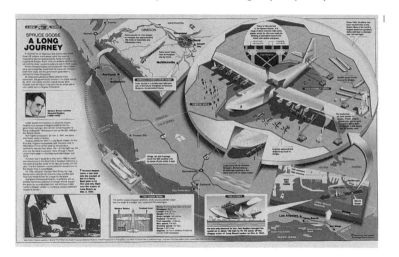

1 Infographic by Nam Nguyeh from 1992. The short-lived career of the largest sea plane in the world, the H-4 (1947).
2 Collage of elements used for the visual representation of statistical information according to the 'Viennese method' of Otto Neurath.

ely, in a single glance'. His aims were lofty and far-reaching: 'The Isotype method may very well become one of the factors that will help to bring about a civilization where all people share a common culture and where the gulf between educated and uneducated will be bridged.'[19] In the end, though, the impact of Neurath's ideas was limited by the fact that his visual vocabulary proved inadequate for depicting more abstract economic circumstances. Nonetheless, thanks to its considerable graphical merit when applied by artists like Gert Arntz, his work remained a source of inspiration for graphic designers. It contributed to the development of pictograms and, indirectly, of the 'infographics' that are becoming increasingly popular in newspapers and magazines.[15] Given the ongoing development of computer graphics programs, moving infographics would seem to be the obvious next step. A good example

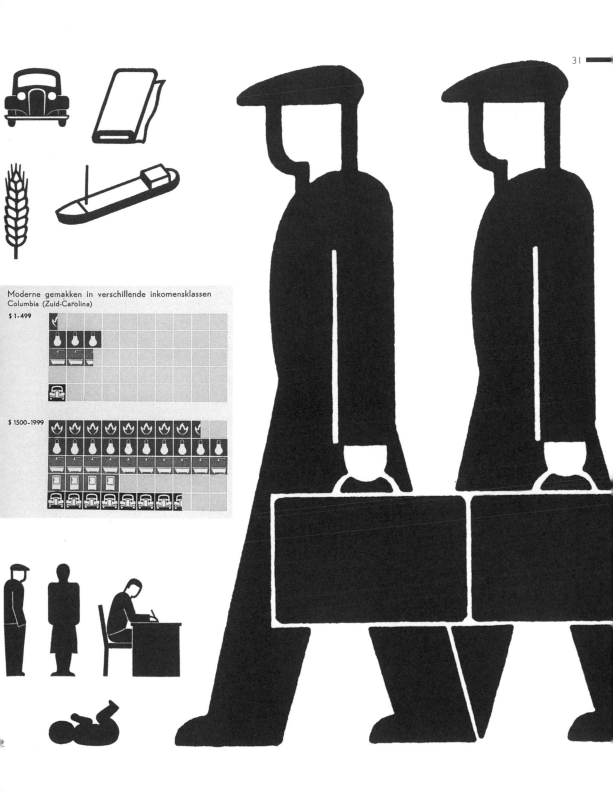

Moderne gemakken in verschillende inkomensklassen
Columbia (Zuid-Carolina)

$ 1-499

$ 1500-1999

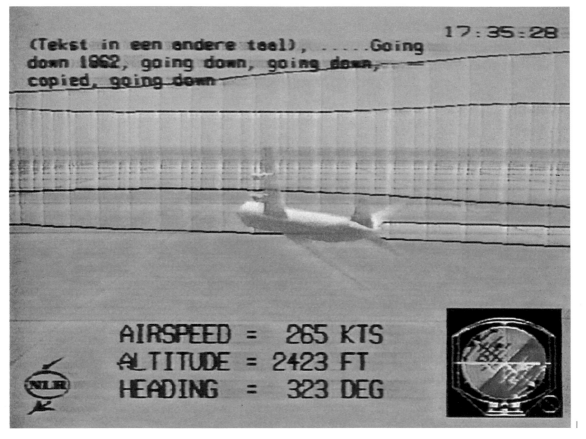

(Tekst in een andere teal), ...Going
down 1862, going down, going down, - =
copied, going down

17:35:28

AIRSPEED = 265 KTS
ALTITUDE = 2423 FT
HEADING = 323 DEG

of this is the computer animation made for the Dutch Civil Aviation Authority, a reconstruction of the ill-fated flight of the Israeli El Al cargo plane on October 4, 1992 up to moment when it crashed onto a suburb on the outskirts of Amsterdam. The animation was based on the audiotape recorded by traffic control at Schiphol Airport and other available details. As a mark of respect, the original dialogue between the captain and traffic control – given in full at the top left of the picture – was spoken by actors. The flight path is visible as a continuous line and the altitude appears as vertical white stripes at fixed intervals. In the lower right-hand corner there is a simulated altitude detector, an important flight instrument. In the excerpt pictured here the aircraft has already lost both starboard motors, a fact of which the crew is as yet unaware.

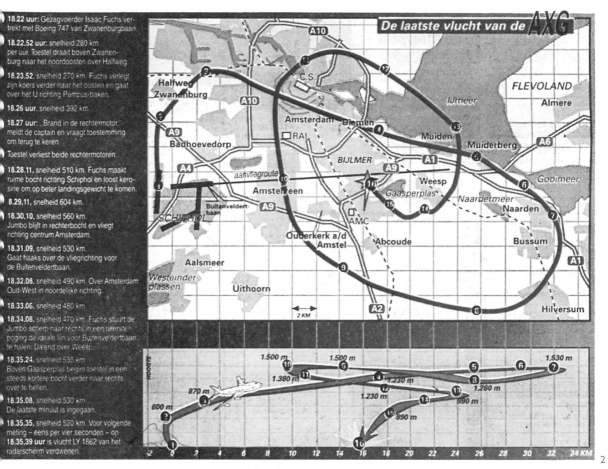

De laatste vlucht van de AXG

18.22 uur: Gezagvoerder Isaac Fuchs vertrekt met Boeing 747 van Zwanenburgbaan.

18.22.52 uur: snelheid 280 km per uur. Toestel draait boven Zwanenburg naar het noordoosten over Halfweg.

18.23.52, snelheid 270 km. Fuchs verlegt zijn koers verder naar het oosten en gaat over het IJ richting Pampus-baken.

18.26 uur, snelheid 392 km.

18.27 uur: ...Brand in de rechtermotor, meldt de captain en vraagt toestemming om terug te keren.

Toestel verliest beide rechtermotoren.

18.28.11, snelheid 510 km. Fuchs maakt ruime bocht richting Schiphol en loost kerosine om op beter landingsgewicht te komen.

8.29.11, snelheid 604 km.

18.30.10, snelheid 560 km. Jumbo blijft in rechterbocht en vliegt richting centrum Amsterdam.

18.31.09, snelheid 530 km. Gaat haaks over de vliegrichting voor de Buitenveldertbaan.

18.32.08, snelheid 490 km. Over Amsterdam Oud-West in noordelijke richting.

18.33.06, snelheid 480 km.

18.34.08, snelheid 470 km. Fuchs stuurt de Jumbo scherp naar rechts in een uiterste poging de ideale lijn voor Buitenveldertbaan te halen. Dalend over Weesp.

18.35.24, snelheid 535 km. Boven Gaasperplas begint toestel in een steeds kortere bocht verder naar rechts over te hellen.

18.35.08, snelheid 530 km. De laatste minuut is ingegaan.

18.35.35, snelheid 520 km. Voor volgende meting – eens per vier seconden – op 18.35.39 uur is vlucht LY 1862 van het radarscherm verdwenen.

2

Excerpt from a computer animation commissioned by the Dutch Civil Aviation Authority. The conversation between the crew and traffic control at Schiphol airport has been synchronized with the image. Infographic from the *Nieuws van de Dag* correlates two graphs (see graph of Napoleonic campaign on p. 29).

The drama created by the addition of sound and movement is not without effect and serves to mask a number of imperfections in the visualization. It is confirmation of the fact that technology is always ahead of design. Yet if we look at a static infographic published in the Dutch evening paper *Nieuws van de Dag* on Tuesday October 6, 1992, two days after the same accident, we see that here the graph makers' skill has compensated for the lack of movement and sound. They have succeeded in creating a total impression in an ingenious combination of map and graph. There is a striking similarity with Minard's graph of Napoleon's march on Moscow a hundred and fifty years earlier. Just as graphic representations are suitable for rendering statistical information about changes, trends, and relationships, cartography depicts parts of our world and the cosmos; pictograms refer succinctly and immediately

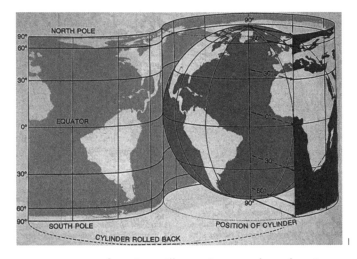

1 The main problem for cartography is how to render spherical information on a flat surface.
2 Front of a London bus. Words and numbers are among the most abstract forms of communication.
3 Product presentation and explanation of operation combined in a single wordless drawing.
4 Diagram devised by Liesbeth Zikkenheimer as a guideline for choosing the appropriate visual media. Classifications include the degree of abstractness and the amount of learning entailed.

to concepts or functions; illustrations, such as drawings and photographs, bring products or product parts to life; and text, finally, is suited to those situations where exact information is crucial.

The choice of visual medium is dictated mainly by how abstract the information is. Highly visual media, like three-dimensional models, film, or photography, are at one end of the visualization spectrum, on the left of Liesbeth Zikkenheimer's chart (taken from this Dutch engineer's manual for producing instructional visual material for immigrants' wives). They are closely related to visible reality and consequently require a relatively short learning process. At the other end of the spectrum, on the right of the chart, are symbols, numbers, and text that are capable of expressing more abstract matters like concepts and ideas. These bear little or no relationship to reality and therefore take

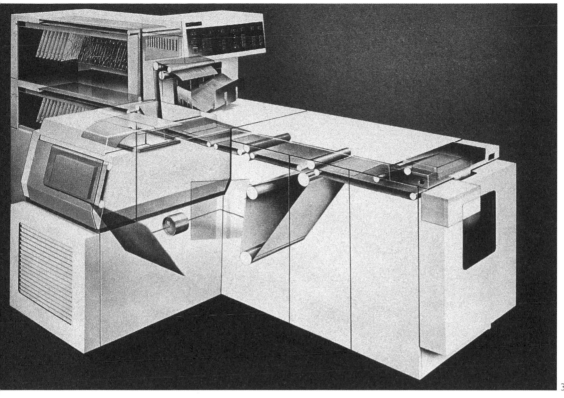

3

4

	Iconic images	Stylized images	Abstract images	Logographic language	Alphabetic language	Letters
refers to	concrete matters	categories	concepts	words	words	sounds
examples	photographs — drawings — cartoons — pictograms — maps — cross-sections — graphs — diagrams			Chinese	English	
incidence	infinite ◄━━━━━━━━━━━━━━► many			10,000 ◄━━━━━━━━━━━━━━► c. 26		
communication	restricted to concrete matters ◄━━━━━━━━━━━━━━━━━━━━► unlimited					
learning	rapid learning (bears close resemblance to reality) ◄━━━► long learning (many symbols and symbol combinations) ◄━━━► short learning					

longer to learn.[28] Nonetheless our understanding of what mode of expression is best suited to a particular type of information is still sketchy. This much is certain: the most effective application, for example in operating instructions, safety instructions, or a control panel, will always consist of a combination of visual media and varying amounts of numbers and words, after which it will be up to layout and detailing to provide the necessary harmonious arrangement and integration. Images provide a different view of things and motivate the user.[29]

1 Effective combination of a diagram and an extremely realistic illustration of the use of commercial timber.
2 Flow diagram from a textbook showing the manufacturing process of a number of metal products.

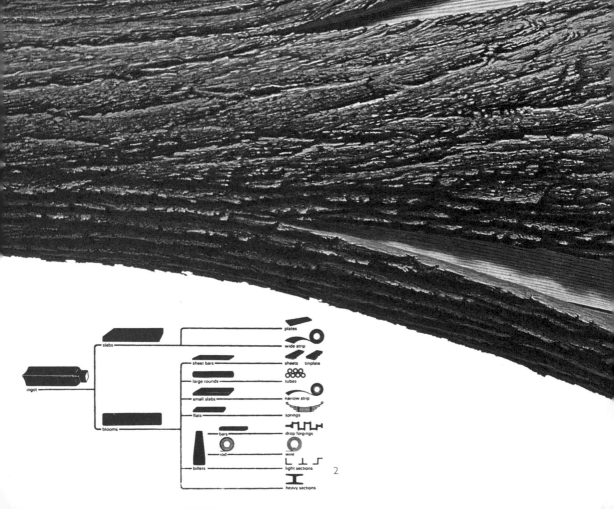

Debarking the log is essential because bark cannot be used for papermaking. However, it is utilized for fuel and as a soil mulch.

The rounded sides, called "slabs," along with other parts of the log not usable as lumber, are sent to the chipper. This picture shows how virtually every piece is utilized efficiently.

The outer portions have the fewest knots, and this "clear" lumber is made into boards or planks from one to three inches in thickness.

Knots increase toward the center of the log since this is the oldest section of the tree, where branches removed during its early life were pruned, leaving knots. This wood is less suitable for boards, so heavier planks and beams are normally sawed from this section.

Veneer for plywood—which is a sandwich of thin veneers—is made by "peeling," or holding a long blade against a rotating log. The core is then treated as though it were a small log, and the excess pieces go on to the chipper.

Graphical Variables

In 1973 the French cartographer Jacques Bertin published a book on the theory of 'graphical variables', *Semiologie Graphique*. In this standard work he defined the basic elements of visual information and their mutual relationships.[2] Bertin distinguished place, size, greyness, texture, orientation, color, and shape. Monotonous but exact numbers made way for visually striking but less precisely observable differences. Indeed, color and form did not indicate quantitative differences and were chosen more or less at random. Nevertheless, they made it possible, for example, to distinguish categories. If Bertin's ideas have met with scant response in his own field of cartography, in the world of graphic design they have remained completely unknown, probably because

1-2
On the left, Bertin's arrangement of 'graphic variables': position, form, size, contrast, 'grain', color, and direction, and right, a variant developed for use by graphic designers.

1

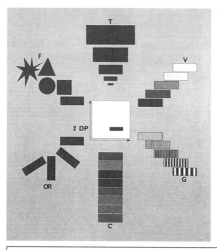

Distinguishing classifies according to category and type	color illustrations column width typeface
Hierarchical classifies according to importance	sequential position (chronology) position on the page (layout) type size type weight line spacing
Supporting accentuating and emphasizing	areas of color and shading lines and boxes symbols, logos, illustrations text attributes (italic, etc.)

2

4

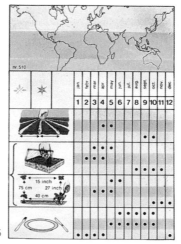

5

6

3 Three examples from Bertin. Left the original sociographical data; right, two different ways of rendering the same *quantitative* data graphically.

4-8

Examples of applications of graphical variables, from left to right: *position* and *size* (of type) in a poster by Jan Tschichold from 1930; *color* (coding) and *form* (symbols). Right-hand page shows examples of *boxes* and *areas of color.*

practical applications are difficult to imagine. In recent years I have attempted to develop a practical variant of Bertin's principles that would provide designers with a set of intelligible and useful guidelines. One can begin by dividing the variables into two categories: hierarchical variables that indicate a difference in importance, and distinguishing variables that indicate a difference in type.

Hierarchical variables can be expressed by means of size and intensity, and distinguishing variables by means of color and form. In addition there are supporting visual elements such as areas of color, lines, and boxes, whose role is to accentuate and organize. Here too it is possible to express differences in importance and type. This breakdown of visual devices makes it possible to analyze in advance the various elements involved in an instruction manual or a control panel, or even a leaflet or

The MIT Press

28 CARLETON ST., CAMBRIDGE, MASS. 02142

TERMS: NET 30 DAYS
NO CASH DISCOUNTS
PAYABLE IN U.S. FUNDS

BOOK RETURNS 190 MERRIMAC ST., LAWRENCE, MASS. 01843

7

2411MO15+

ORIGINAL INVOICE

PAUL MIJKSENAAR
KRALENBEEK 939
AMSTERDAM BIJLMERMEER
HOLLAND NETHERLANDS

S
H
I
P
T
O

MO. DAY. YR.	INVOICE NO.	YOUR ORDER	SPECIAL INSTRUCTIONS		
05NOV74	0128596	OCT2274 ****	FORGN/		

AUTHOR/TITLE		CODE	QTY.	LIST PRICE	DISC.	NET AMOUNT
				RECEIVED PREPAYMENT OF		12.00
GEE/MAN MADE	P	GMM	1	4.95	NET	4.95
WURMAN/MAN MADE PHILADEL	P	WMPT	1	3.95	NET	3.95
WURMAN/YELLOW PAGES	P	WYP	1	1.95	NET	1.95
POSTAGE/PD/ON/PREPAID/OR		9003				1.15

8

toepassing:
7.6.1 - in geval van overlijden van verzekerde, het bepaalde in 7.2.2 tot en met 7.2.5 en 7.3.1 tot en met 7.3.8
7.6.2 - in geval van opsporen (6.7.2), het bepaalde in 7.2.: tot en met 7.2.4 en 7.3.1 tot en met 7.3.8.

12 Uitkering

12.2 - De maximale uitkering voor reiskosten voor zieken huisbezoek (6.4.5) is ƒ 500,- per polis.
12.3 - Vergoeding vindt plaats onder aftrek van besparin gen, restituties en dergelijke. Op verblijfskosten zal wegen bespaarde kosten van normaal levensonderhoud een vast aftrek worden toegepast van 10%.

Rubriek bagage

1 Begripsomschrijvingen

In de polis en voorwaarden wordt verstaan onder:
1.7 - **bagage:** tot eigen gebruik door verzekerde meegeno men, dan wel binnen de geldigheidsduur van de verzekerin; tegen ontvangstbewijs vooruit- of nagezonden voorwerpei (waaronder begrepen kostbaarheden en reisdocumenten) echter:
1.7.1 - winter- en onderwatersportartikelen, ook indien ir het buitenland gehuurd, alleen voor de verzekerde voor wi het sportrisico is meeverzekerd
1.7.2 - geld, waaronder te verstaan gangbare munten, bank biljetten en cheques, alleen indien geld is meeverzekerd
1.8 - **kostbaarheden:** horloges (waaronder mee te verstaar horlogebanden en -kettingen), sieraden (waaronder te ver

8

magazine, and to assign them suitable variables. The matrix developed for this purpose is illustrated below, filled in with the kind of elements one might find in a handbook. Using this method one could design the legend before the map, the buttons and meters before the control panel, and the operating instructions before the appliance. Only then would the actual information or functions be worked out. Interactive media – that is to say electronic information systems – even make it possible to simulate use in advance, thereby enabling manufacturers to test the various functions on a simulated control panel displayed on a color screen before embarking on the actual design process. As subjects key in the imaginary buttons, the screen shows what would happen in reality. The designer gains a better understanding of the machine while the manufacturer saves both time and money on the design process.

1 Example of how the distinguishing and hierarchical variables from the plan on page 38 could be used in the typographic translation of the editorial elements of a magazine.
2 The sequence of stages passed through in the act of reading.

Hiërarchical variabels	A	B	C	D		
+4			title		1	stage 1 **Comprehension**
+3	headline	sub-title				a position; sequence (time)
+2	intro	headings				b position; direction
+1			text attribute			stage 2 **Assimilation**
0			flat type	illustrations		c type size
−1	summary, facts, etc.	lists, tables, etc.	caption	repeat of title		d type contrast (bold/light; upright/slanted)
−2				page number		stage 3 **Recognition**
−3			notes			e column layout
	A	**B**	**C**	**D**		f typesetting; line spacing
						g typeface

Distinguising variables

2

Gewässer:

3 In this legend all the topographical symbols have been incorporated into an imaginary landscape.

When the designer eventually comes to design such pretested visual elements, he or she will have to deal with the meaning a user will assign to them. The results of ergonomic research – ergonomics sometimes overlaps our discipline but is more concerned with creating favourable conditions – can be marshalled into a rough order of priority (see right-hand plan opposite). Oddly enough, it appears that many graphic designers are in the habit of working through this plan from bottom to top rather than the other way around. For example, they first spend a lot of time deciding on the typeface, or – more futile still – they add another one to the estimated 60,000 already in existence. The upshot is that they frequently do not get around to the most essential element at the top of the plan: time. This concept is defined as sequence (as in the pages in a book or on a screen) and as reading or viewing direction.

4

5

4 Typefaces are more suited to aesthetic image creation than to the representation of functional differences.

5 Redesigned by Erik Terlouw in 1986, the Dutch newspaper *Trouw* uses only one typeface (Frutiger) but it rings the changes by employing several contrasting variants and a variety of type sizes.

Time, in the sense of sequence, plays a major role in the design of instruction leaflets (what should we tell the user first?) and more especially of interactive media. Users are unable to flick through screen pages as they can with a book.

Time in the sense of viewing direction is important in such activities as reading a newspaper page, filling out a form, and using a control panel. Time offers architects, film directors, novelists, and exhibition designers the opportunity to create space, build up suspense, and tell a story.

One way of creating suspense, for example, is to combine the variable 'time' with 'size'. Information that appears later on can still produce a shock by virtue of its size.

Since I fail to see why this could not be achieved with graphical work (El Lissitsky spoke of a 'bioscopic book' as long ago as 1923),[13] I can only assume that graphic designers lack a sense of drama, a conclusion that tallies with the observation of a certain design manager who remarked that he seldom ran into designers at the theater.

The lack of a 'scenario' in many graphic designs is perfectly reflected in the frequently misconceived – because ineffective – use of transparent paper, die cutting, and fold-out pages in books, and the placement – or rather burying – of the captions to illustrations.

In children's books and picture books like Guy Billout's *Waiting*, suspense and climax are provided by the element of *time* (sequence).

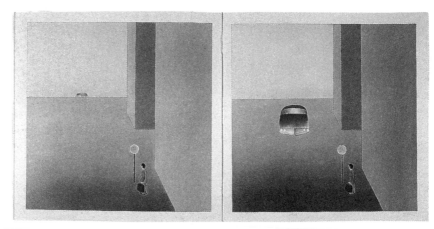

Three Cheers for the Everyday

Design is generally assumed to be an offshoot of the visual arts. There is undoubtedly some common ground in the use of visual devices, and it is also true that many designers draw their inspiration from the visual arts. Yet there are many other possible sources of inspiration available, such as music and nature. (Conversely, there are plenty of examples of artists who look to technology for inspiration.)

Designers of graphic consumer products would do well to allow themselves to be influenced by the visual riches of everyday products. Yet most of them — like most art historians, incidentally — experience such objects as banal, tacky, and vulgar.

In my opinion, this attitude causes them to overlook many interesting,

From a French manual for pruning fruit trees

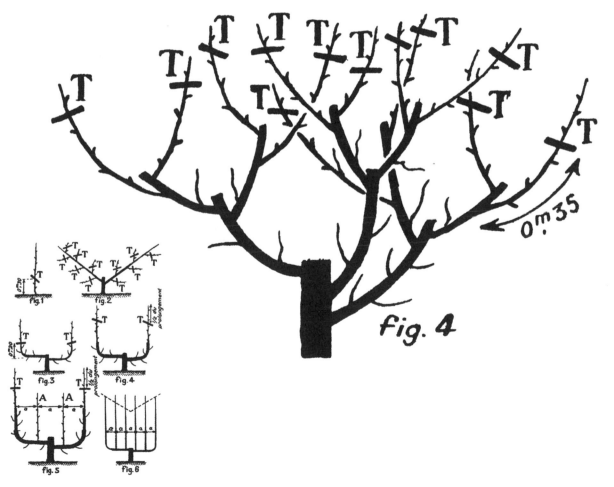

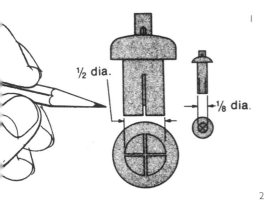

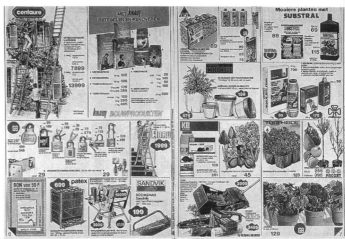

1 A hand holding a pencil draws attention to an important detail in a technical catalogue.
2 Mail order catalogue in which the layout attempts to evoke the atmosphere of a flea market.
3 Creative design of license plates in the US draws attention to the driver's home state.

striking, and extremely useful solutions. This is not, of course, a plea on behalf of indiscriminate imitation of everyday objects; but as a source of inspiration they can sometimes rival and always supplement their lofty counterparts in the arts.

5 Label on a box of screws.
6 The *Bibendum* mascot was
based on an idea of André
Michelin.

Experiment or Craftsmanship

We are inundated with the results of scientific research, yet a depressingly small amount of this ever finds its way into the design of visual information. In the first instance the blame lies with the researchers themselves. The average research report is totally impenetrable to the layman, while the conclusions and recommendations – when they exist – are hedged round with enough reservations to boggle the mind of the practically inclined designer. They would not be out of place among the fine print of an insurance policy.

This is the problem faced by the handful of designers who take the trouble to gather knowledge. A substantially larger group of designers, however, has a very different set of priorities: self-expression, creativity,

'I am firmly convinced that creativity lies not in finding new material but in rearranging what already exists.'

Pascal, 1623-1662

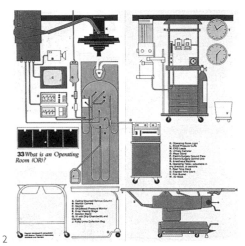

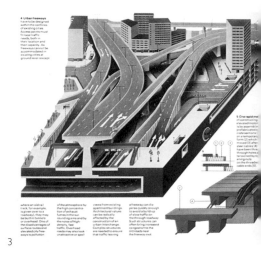

33 What is an Operating Room (OR)?

1 In LEGO directions, one can count every stud.
2 Excerpt from Saul Wurman's 'Access' series which involves a step-by-step visualization of hospital procedures.
3 Technical illustration from Mitchell Beazley's *Man & Machines*, a field of specialization that is not taught in the Netherlands.

and experimentation are a few of their most important motivations. Conspicuously absent from this catalogue is innovation.

A teacher at one of the Dutch fine arts colleges gave his students the task of designing a keyboard for a pocket calculator the size of a credit card. The underlying idea was to confront these students of the applied arts almost unobtrusively with several stringent preconditions, the most important in this particular case being the very tiny area onto which they had to fit all the information. The fact that a number of students thought they could get away with handing in a design the size of a large menu is surprising enough. But that they should have dismissed the teacher's objections that they had not stuck to the brief as 'nit-picking' is nothing short of alarming.

Paul Maas's illustration for Shell; the height of an oilrig is compared not only to the Eiffel Tower but also to Dutch landmarks.

Such attitudes tend to undermine craftsmanship and insight into the communicative task of a product: utility and reliability. This general lack of interest in the content of information is one of the reasons why the Netherlands, with the exception of the work of the Das brothers, has almost no tradition in the area of scientific and technical illustration. This applies equally to educational design – works of reference, textbooks, popular science books – in short, to the design of visual information. Those who nurture this one-sided interest in form are often teachers or, worse still, members of government-appointed advisory committees.[30] As such, I fear that we are unlikely to see an early return to a degree of balance between content and form, with room for satisfying functionality.

Trends

The large-scale introduction of microelectronics in just about every product you can think of has led to a staggering rise in the number of functions per product. The upshot, according to Piet Westendorp, a researcher at Delft University, is that the operation of even the most straightforward of products, such as a wristwatch or a radio, is more complicated than ever before. One of the greatest stumbling blocks for today's consumer in this respect is the programmable video recorder. The end result of this development is ever-thicker instruction manuals, increasingly complex control panels, and overcrowded maps.

It is time to reverse the order in which we do things: to begin by designing the control panel, the instructions, the legend, or the signage

1 Combination of comic strip elements and aerial view in a Dutch Air Force recruitment pamphlet.

2-7 The multiplicity of functions performed by modern appliances makes ease of use, and hence clear instructions, essential.

2 Yet the design of products that are 'simple to operate' is still in its infancy

3 First components of a universal visual language devised by industrial designer John Dreyfuss.

4 Film-style sequence from the Het Beste Autohandboek.

5 Close-up of a component in instructions for a Husqvarna sewing machine.

6 Comic-strip approach to illustrations in a Dutch sign language handbook.

7 Overview of internationally famous towers in a fictional city center. Part of an infographic by J. Grimwade in The Times (London).

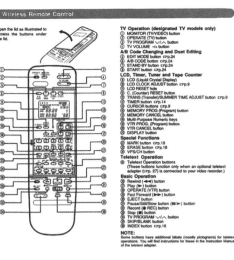

2

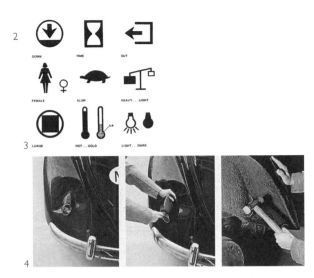

3

4

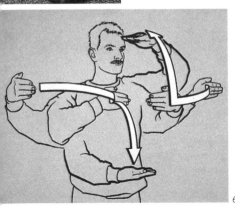

5

6

7

system and tailoring them to the users – their dimensions, their capabilities, and their limitations. And only then to design the product.

At the same time, the development of a visual language and accompanying grammar begun by Otto Neurath and continued by industrial designer John Dreyfuss in his *Symbol Sourcebook* (1967) should be resumed.[5]

Visual information makes full use of new visual forms borrowed from photography, film, and not least from comic strips and technical illustrations. Think, for example, of close-ups, cropped pictures, suggested movement, perspective, and projection.

The current trend in safety instructions aimed at aircraft passengers will serve as an example. Until now most instructions have consisted of a

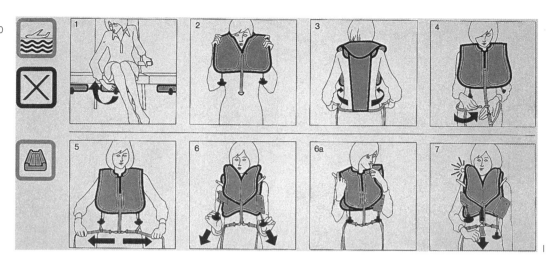

card showing a series of simplified illustrations with all superfluous details omitted for the sake of clarity. The English art historian Ernst Gombrich doubts whether a passenger involved in an emergency landing on water would be able to tie on the life jacket on the basis of these illustrations.[8] (Personally I am more inclined to lay the blame for this particular problem at the door of the life-jacket's designer.)

There are two current trends in this area. The first is a German proposal for a standardized visual language. The advantage for passengers would be that the same visual language would be used throughout the world, regardless of aircraft type or airline.

The second trend takes the opposite, realistic approach and uses either a comic strip or a series of staged photographs. The drawback of photography – it shows too many irrelevant details and is unable to

1 The safety instruction card referred to by Ernst Gombrich
2 Proposed standardized safety instructions for aircraft.
3 Detail from Swissair's photographic instruction card.

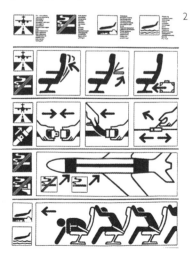

4

emphasize the important ones – is obvious here: only a close-up makes it clear that passengers are not permitted to smoke standing up. Elaborating on this trend, Swissair, Lufthansa and other airlines are replacing the usual demonstration by cabin personnel with a video animation shown on board the aircraft. As the excerpt below shows, all extraneous detail has been omitted. In addition, slow-motion has been used so that consecutive images overlap, the idea being that passengers will be able to follow the sequence of actions more easily.

Excerpt from the colored, comic-strip-style drawings used by British Airways. Still from Swissair's video animation.

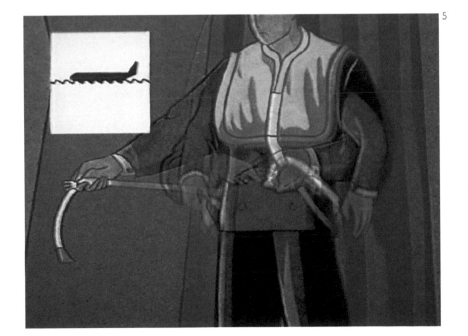

5

Form follows content

Around 1873 one of the Netherlands most famous writers, Multatuli (pseudonym for Douwes Dekker), wrote: 'Endeavour – with most diligent labour, O aspiring artist! – to master content. The form will rise to meet you'.

Although he was speaking of literature and not, like Henry Greenough, of architecture, Multatuli illustrated this maxim with an example that is nonetheless equally relevant to product design. The discussion about form and content reminded him of the 'beggar who debates whether he would keep his gold in a purse or a pouch . . . if he had any gold!'[18] Ideas are all and they are in short supply, according to Multatuli. Without content there is no form. The major part of this book has been devoted to content, to the 'idea', because it is in understanding and interpreting this that design begins.[29] It is nice to know that even before the American Sullivan made his famous pronouncement, a Dutch writer had already managed to state the issue so succinctly.

...Between heaven and earth...
(crossroads near Venice)

Regarding Training and Designers

I have the impression that design has come under increasing pressure from disciplines that work with seemingly tangible and measurable data. However important these may be for future designers, the binding element in product design is the act of shaping. It is this that provides the 'look' that consumers recognize as a mark of quality and integrity and it is the only part of the design process capable of supplying wit, youth and gaiety (to quote Hartmut Esslinger[1] of *frogdesign*) and aesthetic satisfaction. It is the task of scientists and designers to uncover the many still-hidden but unmistakably operative laws of design and to develop tools designers can use to give shape to their ideas.

Clients have always been the motivating force spurring designers to garner knowledge, invent models and methods, and devise solutions. The best designs come about in collaboration with critical clients who give careful consideration to the often subjective arguments advanced by designers and who are not prepared to take things at face value. One example of a client acting as a guiding force is Schiphol Airport. From the very beginning, management insisted that a clear distinction be maintained between rational and functional aspects on the one hand and aesthetic quality on the other. With such an approach, the otherwise inevitable discussions about beautiful and ugly can be put off until after the content has been established in principle, thereby solving a problem that often bedevils and sometimes paralyzes the design profession.

It cannot be the object of science to provide recipes or instant answers. That would, in any case, be impossible. Nor does it make much sense to study only brilliant examples, for the results of imitation are usually profoundly tedious.[1] Education can help students to acquire knowledge and insight and, to quote the Dutch designer Walter Nikkels, 'stimulate ingenuity, creativity, curiosity and unremitting diligence in the field of techniques and materials.'[29]

Sources

1   Albers, J., *Search Versus Re-Search*, Hartford 1969
2   Bertin, J., *Sémiologie Graphique*, Paris 1973
3   Bevers, A. M., *Vorm en Functie: Esthetiek van de sociale relaties*, Intreerede Erasmus Universiteit, Rotterdam 1991
4   Bilderman, A., "The Playfair Enigma," in: *Information Design Journal*, 1990, no. 1, pp. 3–25
5   Dreyfuss, H., *Symbol Sourcebook*, New York 1967
6   Garland, K., *Mr Beck's Underground Map*, Harrow Weald, 1994
7   Giedion, S., *Mechanization Takes Command*, New York 1969
8   Gombrich, E., "Pictorial Instructions," in: H. Barlow (ed.) *Images and Understanding*, Cambridge 1990
9   Groot, A. de, "Rationeel en functioneel bouwen 1840–1920," catalogue: *Het Nieuwe Bouwen: Voorgeschiedenis*, Delft 1982
10 Heskett, J., *Industrial Design*, London 1980, 1987
11 Huisman, J., 'Artikelen van frogdesign laten zich graag strelen,' in: *de Volkskrant*, Semptember 1992, supplement 'Vervolgens,' p. 11
12 Janson, H. W., *Form follows function - or does it?*, Maarssen 1982
13 Kinross, R., *Modern Typography: An essay in critical history*, London 1992
14 Mijksenaar, P. P., 'Andrew Holmes,' in: *Grensoverschrijdingen / Trans-border design*, Kalender Mart. Spruijt, Amsterdam 1991/92
15 Mijksenaar, P. P., 'Infographics,' in: Jaarverslag 1991 *Perscombinatie*, Amsterdam 1992
16 Mijksenaar, P. P., 'Typografie bij bewegwijzering. Of: de strijd tussen esthetiek en rekenliniaal,' in: *Graficus Revue*, 1971, no. 3, pp. 12–30
17 Mijksenaar, P. P. en Vroman, R., 'London Transport Map: A Delft Project,' in: *Typos*, 1983, no. 6, pp. 36–40
18 Multatuli, *Ideeën van Multatuli*, zesde bundel, Amsterdam 1987
19 Neurath, O., *De moderne mensch ontstaat: Een reportage van vreugde en vrees*, Amsterdam 1940
20 Norman, D. A., *The Psychology of Everyday Things*, New York, 1988
21 Owen, C., 'Style, Styling and Design: Beyond Formalism,' in: *Design Processes Newsletter*, 1991, no. 3, pp. 7–10
22 Passini, R., *Wayfinding in Architecture*, New York 1984
23 Patton, P., 'Up from flatland,' in: *The New York Times Magazine*, 19 January 1992, pp. 28–31, 61
24 Tufte, E. R., *Envisioning Information*, Cheshire 1990
25 Tufte, E. R., *The Visual Display of Quantitative Information*, Cheshire 1983
26 Wildbur, P., *Information Graphics*, Houten 1989
27 Wolff, M. de, 'Over Henry van de Velde,' in: *de Volkskrant*, 11 September 1992
28 Zikkenheimer, L., *Beeldmateriaal en Buitenlandse vrouwen*, The Hague 1986
29 Advertisement Ministry of WVC, *Adformatie*, 15 August 1991
30 *Visies rond educatief vormgeven en illustreren*, Den Bosch 1991

Illustrations*

p. 2   Manual *Canon Laserprinter LBP8-II*
p. 4   Kooy, H. van der, in: *Informatie openbaar vervoer in Amsterdam*, Gemeente Vervoerbedrijf Amsterdam March 1989
p. 4   With permission of the © Metropolitan Transportation Authority 1987
p. 4   With permission of the © Metropolitan Transportation Authority, Revised Fall 1980
p. 5   Tati, J., *Mon Oncle*, 1958
p. 6   Beck, H., Map: *London Underground 97/E/858*, 1949
p. 6   Mijksenaar, P. P., *London Transport Map, A Delft Project*, Delft 1983
p. 7   Holmes, A., in: *Busroutes en bezienswaardigheden in het centrum van London*, London Transport, 1993–1994
p. 7   Tufte, E. R., Visual Explanations
p. 7   Morton–Thiokol, *Report of the Presidential commission of the Spae Shuttle Challenger Accident*
p. 8   Derwigs, J., in: J. Derwigs and E. Mattie, *Amsterdamse School*, Amsterdam 1991, photograph 30
p. 10 *Menoor wijst u de weg*
p. 11 *Swatch horloges*, Switzerland
p. 11 G. Berlijn, *Wereldtentoonstellingen, Kerstnummer Grafisch Nederland 1991*, Amstelveen 1991
p. 11 Source unknown

Explanation of symbols in the first Michelin guide of 1900.

* As far as could be established.

p. 12 Delft University of Technology, Faculty of Industrial Design

p. 13 *Volvo instructions*, Helmond

p. 14 *Volvo instructions*, Helmond

p. 14 *Bosch Travelpilot IDS, Doelgericht naar uw bestemming*

p. 15 *Philips steam iron*

p. 16 Manour, J., *Clipper Ship Cowper*, 1854

p. 16 Heskett, J., *Industrial Design*, London 1980, 1987, p. 39

p. 18 Saroglia, F., 1964

p. 18 Treumann, O.

p. 20 *Swatch watch*, Switzerland

p. 20 *Douwe Egberts gifts 1993*, Utrecht 1993

p. 21 Bayer, H., *Bauhaus–Archiv*, Berlin 1925

p. 21 Sandberg, W., *Experimenta typographica 2*, Cologne 1969

p. 22 Moore, R. L. and A. W. Christie, 'Research on Traffic Signs,' in: *Engineering for Traffic Conference*, July 1963, p. 116

p. 23 *Michelin*, according to *Michelin Guide Rouge, Offert gracieusement aux chauffeurs*, 1990 edition, p. 191.

p. 24 Toyota, advertisement

p. 25 *Siemens Bildzeichen Hausgeräte*, August 1981

p. 25 Dutch Railways, *Spoorstijl*, 1988

p. 26 Dawson, J. D., 'Layers of life at the top,' in: *National Geographic*, 1991, vol. 180, no. 6, p. 91

p. 27 *Vruchten: Praktisch Koken*, Amsterdam 1983, pp. 34–35

p. 27 Mitchell, J., *Man & Machines. The Mitchell Beazley Joy of Knowledge Library*, London 1977, pp. 248–249

p. 28 Oresme, N., c. 1350

p. 28 Playfair, W., 1786

p. 29 Minard, C.J., *Bibliothèque de l'Ecole Nationale des Ponts et Chaussées*, 1869, Paris

p. 29 Nightingale, F., 1855

p. 30 Nguyeh, N., *Pruce Goose - A Long Journey*, 1992

p. 31 Neurath, O., *De moderne mensch ontstaat: Een reportage van vreugde en vrees*, Amsterdam 1940, p. 120

p. 31 Arntz, G. and K. Broos, *Symbolenboek voor onderwijs en statistiek: 1928–1965*, Amsterdam 1979

p. 32 Animation NLR, 1992: courtesy of the Dutch Civil Aviation Authority, Hoofddorp

p. 33 Steenbergen, M., 'Drie minuten,' in: *De Telegraaf / De Courant / Nieuws van de Dag*, 6 October 1992, p. 5

p. 34 Richard E. Harrison, in: *Scientific American*, 1975, vol. 233, no. 5, p. 121

p. 35 Zikkenheimer, L., *Beeldmateriaal en Buitenlandse vrouwen*, The Hague 1986

p. 36 Ketchum, M., *The Secret Life of the Forest*, New York 1970, pp. 98–99

p. 36 Rankin, J.A., *Workshop processes and materials for mechnanical engineering technicians*

p. 38 Bertin, J., *Sémiologie Graphique*, Paris 1973, p. 43

p. 38 Tschichold, J., 1930

p. 38 Seed packet

p. 39 Bertin, J., *Sémiologie Graphique*, Paris 1973, pp. 116, 133, 137

p. 39 *Invoice*, The MIT Press, Cambridge, Mass. 1974

p. 39 European Insurance Company, Amsterdam

p. 40 *Legenda Topografische kaarten*, 1:25000, Hessischer Landesvervessungsamt, 1975

p. 41 Parry, J., *Fantasy of a Bill Sticker*, 1835, Victoria & Albert Museum, London

p. 41 *Trouw*, 22 October 1986, p. 1

p. 42 Billout, G., *Wachten*, The Hague 1973

p. 43 Pont, A., *Taille Fruitière par l'image*, Paris 1948, pp. 25, 55

p. 44 *Southco Fastener*, Handbook, Concordville

p. 44 *Bricopub*, Evere, 4 September 1986

p. 45 Cauzard, D., J. Perret, Y. Ronin, *Images de marques, marques d'images*, Paris 1988, p. 108

p. 46 *LEGO*, Denmark

p. 46 Wurman, R.S., *Medical Access*, Access Press

p. 46 Mitchell, J., *Man & Machines, The Mitchell Beazley Joy of Knowledge Library*, London 1977, p. 185

p. 47 Maas, P., in: Shellvenster 1993

p. 48 Basis 2000, in: *Kijk, de Koninklijke Luchtmacht: Op weg naar 2000*, The Hague

p. 49 *Instructions HR–D560EG/E video cassette recorder*, JVC, 1991

Explanation of symbols in the 1992 Michelin guide

Repas

enf. 55

p. 49 *Het Beste Autohandboek, Vraagbaak voor gebruik en onderhoud,* Amsterdam 1972
p. 49 *Sewing machine instructions,* Husqvarna
p. 49 Stichting Vi-taal, The Hague 1993
p. 49 Grimwade, J., 'Towers of power,' in: *The Times,* 11 October 1985
p. 50 *Safety instructions B747,* 1989
p. 50 Klaus G. Hofe, development and design; Jack Stachowsky, realisation and drawing, safety instructions
p. 50 *Safety instructions A310, Swissair*
p. 51 *Safety instructions Boeing 737-400,* British Airways, 1992
p. 51 *Safety on board,* courtesy of Swissair
p. 52 In the vicinity of Venice
p. 54 © *Michelin,* according to *Michelin Guide Rouge, Offert gracieusement aux chauffeurs,* 1900 edition, p. 399.
p. 55 © *Michelin* , according to *Michelin Guide Rouge,* 1997 edition
p. 56 Goods van sticker, British Railways

Unless otherwise indicated, all materials were furnished by the Stichting Archief Paul Mijksenaar.

Label for goods wagons
(British Rail)

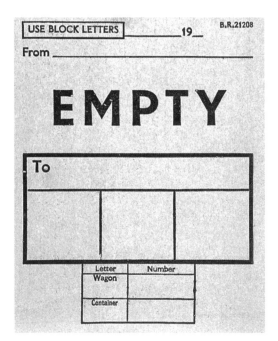

Text editor: Ed van Hinte
Design: Bureau Mijksenaar, Amsterdam
DTP: Lauran Schijvens, Rotterdam
Lithography and printing: Snoeck Ducaju, Ghent

Visual Function is first published in the English language in North and South America by Princeton Architectural Press, 37 East Seventh Street, New York, NY 10003.
Visual Function is first published in all other countries by 010 Publishers, Watertorenweg 180, 3063 HA Rotterdam, The Netherlands.

© 1997 Paul Mijksenaar and 010 Publishers (www.archined.nl/010)
ISBN 1-56898-118-X